C000221777

PHILIP ASTLEY

WHO
?
WAS

WHO WAS . . . ?

PHILIP ASTLEY

THE INVENTOR OF THE CIRCUS

BY **NELL STROUD**

ILLUSTRATED BY **JAMES NUNN**

✳ SHORT BOOKS

First published in 2003 by
Short Books
15 Highbury Terrace
London N5 1UP

10 9 8 7 6 5 4 3 2 1

A CIP catalogue record for this book
is available from the British Library.

ISBN 1-904095-31-3

Printed in Great Britain by
Bookmarque Ltd, Croydon, Surrey

For Jimmy Joe

CHAPTER ONE

It is a stormy winter night. Trees whip against the dark sky like rags. Philip Astley, the hero of our story, sixteen years old, is riding like the devil on a wild horse to Coventry. His black hair is stuck to his forehead, his eyes shine, his lips are pressed together – cold with fear. Schoolboy no more, wood-working apprentice no more – he is wide awake, out in the night on his own, running away from home.

The horse's neck and head stream out in front of him. Mud and stones from the road splash its legs and chest. The mud covers Philip too – his breeches, his leather shoes, and his terrified, exhausted face. Tears cling to his cheeks in the driving rain. His arms and shoulders ache where the horse pulls and pulls on the reins.

Above him the night sky is thick and black, like dirty oil. There are no stars and no moon. Philip and the galloping horse are all alone on the empty road. He has lost his way and only the horse knows where they are going. He is frightened that the horse will stumble and fall, and then gallop away, and then he will be at the mercy of cruel highwaymen and runaway convicts and all the other people who only come out under cover of darkness. All Philip can do is trust the horse. He longs for his warm bed. But it's no use. This isn't a dream.

Earlier that evening, he had shouted at his father, scorned his poor mother, said things for which he would never be forgiven. And now he is wretched and defiant. With each stride of the horse he is carried further and further from home; with each stride of the horse his chances of going home, of being forgiven, grow less. He imagines his father raging, his mother crying. He cannot go back, he can never go back; they

hate him, he is sure of that. To go back would be to give in. He has come this far, down an empty road. It would be more difficult now to go back than to carry on. After such a row – how could he ever be forgiven? His mother would cry, but his father would blaze like an angry bonfire, burn up Philip's words and turn him back into a little boy. And he *isn't* a boy, he tells himself, he is a man.

As the horse's hooves drum on the stony road he

chants in time with them, under his breath – never go back, never go back, never go back.

So in a terrible fit of fear, and longing for the bright fireplace and hot dinner of home, Philip clings to the horse's mane and snatches at the slippery reins. The horse is his anchor, his salvation, his future.

CHAPTER TWO

Philip Astley was born in 1742 in Newcastle-under-Lyme. His father, Edward, was a cabinet-maker – a tall, strong man with black hair and a fierce temper.

As a baby, Philip was small, thin and wriggly. He hated being cuddled. He wanted to crawl on the floor, drag himself up on to the wooden chairs and benches in the kitchen. He never stopped wailing and crying, never for a moment let his mother rest.

But he grew up to be tough and strong, without the bandy legs and soft bones of his friends, who had rickets. And he never caught the dreaded smallpox, a disease a bit like chickenpox, but much more deadly. Philip, from a very young age, knew that it was not his lot to lie in bed with a temperature.

His restlessness made his mother tired and dis-tressed. One morning, in despair, she took him into her husband's carpentry workshop.

'There', she cried, 'you look after the child, for I do declare he has quite worn me out.'

And so, by the time he was six, Philip was spending much of each day with his father, learning the skills of carpentry. His parents weren't poor, but nor were they grand, with time and money for games and trav-el and rich foods. They were tradespeople. They made things to sell. And although for some years in his boy-hood Philip also went to school to learn to read and write, he knew that he was always destined to become a carpenter's apprentice, so that he too could learn a trade and make a living.

It was not long before he began to slip out of the workshop when his father wasn't looking.

He had made friends with the ostler who looked after the horses of the travellers staying at the inn next door. One day, when a lot of coaches arrived at the same time and the ostler was rushing around making sure that all the horses were properly fed and cared for, he gave Philip a brush and some vague instructions.

'Don't go near the little chestnut on the end, mind, he kicks like a donkey.'

Philip was intrigued by this kicking donkey-horse. He walked up to it, slowly, carefully, step by step, but the horse stood quiet. He saw no reason to stay away from the animal.

'You are a good horse, donkey-horse, I know you are. The ostler must be mad, or perhaps he imagines things.'

The horse just stared at the little boy with his black sooty eyes. Philip decided that this was the horse he would brush down. Philip was only nine years old, and he couldn't reach the top of the horse's back. Undefeated, he climbed up the horse's back legs, and stood on its hocks. The horse did not stir.

When the ostler returned he could not believe what he was seeing.

'I swear the child is a devil. That horse is mean and vicious, and yet with Philip it is as gentle as a lamb.'

And the next time he saw Philip's father, he told him, 'On my mother's life, your son has a rare gift.'

But Philip's father was not much impressed by his

son's diabolical gifts. As far as he was concerned, Philip's future was in the workshop. He dragged his son from the stables, and told him firmly that he was forbidden to go back to the inn. He banged his fist on the table. He was very, very angry, and Philip was frightened of his anger.

And yet Philip could find no pleasure in woodworking. The constant sanding and polishing of other people's ornate tables was boring. He wanted to be doing something that had his name all over it, that dazzled and shone. Philip Astley the great! He said to himself. I am the great Philip Astley. Great for what, though? He had no idea, but he knew that he didn't want to be the creator of a table in the corner of some dusty drawing-room. His parents had saved hard to provide for him, but Philip was blind to this, and ungrateful. He had no time for their comfortable, respectable world. It was lifeless and dull.

It seemed as though everything interesting happened outside. Great rumbling wagons, the mighty stagecoaches, the dainty gigs and flies passed by the windows of the workshop on their way to the great city of Manchester in the north, or Birmingham in the south, and Philip was tantalised by the shadows they cast across the workbench, and the sounds of the shouts and calls of their drivers and passengers. There were so many things to be done, to be found out, and Philip felt that if he didn't go soon, then the rest of the world would get there first.

He brooded and scowled, and his temper worsened. As he grew from a boy to a man he began to realise that his father could not scare him any more with his tempers, and he set his mind on leaving.

***

On a cold winter's day in 1759, Philip was with his father when he heard a commotion in the street outside – carriages clattering over cobblestones, horses galloping, men shouting and laughing. People were gathering to go to the horse fair at Coventry.

Philip was chiselling a small dovetail joint in the

arm of a delicate mahogany chair. He felt an odd sensation welling up inside, like he was daring himself to do something terrible. He felt that he was standing on the edge of a cliff, and that any minute he would hurl himself off.

He looked across the warm workshop at his father, who was concentrating on carving a tiny horse's head on the edge of a table leg. Philip knew that now was the moment to shatter for ever his father's control. He put down his chisel on the gleaming table top.

'I... I am going to Coventry, father. Don't try and stop me. My mind's quite made up.'

His father didn't look up.

'Don't be silly, Philip. What good would a horse fair be to you? What would you learn there?'

'I don't know. But I am going to go, and I am going to go now.'

Philip was short of breath and there was fear in his throat and chest. With every word he committed himself to something he couldn't see, only sense, something full of light and movement, faraway in the future, and faraway from the snug workshop. His father looked down again at his work and said gently, 'What would you *do*, though, Philip?'

'I am good with horses father, you know I am. I have a talent there. You have heard the ostler talking, over the years, haven't you?'

'That man is full of gin. You are a stupid boy to listen to his counsel!' Edward instantly regretted his words. He knew that Philip wasn't stupid. The boy was the image of himself at that age – wilful, a dreamer, and as strong as an ox. But he didn't want him to join a world of travellers and vagrants. He wanted him to grow up a respectable young man.

And yet Philip's constant complaints, his restlessness, his lack of concentration, had gradually worn away at Edward's fatherly patience, and there were times when he almost began to despise his son's ingratitude for the comfortable home he had provided him with. That was why he had called Philip stupid. He was stupid to listen to the drunk next door.

'I am *not* stupid! *Don't* call me stupid! I hate you

and I hate this work!' Philip was terrified by his own words.

His father was too shocked for a moment to speak. He turned away, unable to look at the boy that he had loved so dearly for sixteen years.

'Well, Philip, if that is really how you feel, you must go. If this life is not good enough for you, then go. Find something better, leave now, immediately, but understand this: if you go now, I will never want to see you again.'

Edward prayed in his heart that Philip would not leave; he hated himself for his harsh words. Philip, for his part, knew that if he didn't leave now, right now, and set off with the strangers outside, then he would never go, and his father would have won.

Tears filled Philip's eyes as he looked around the workshop for the last time. He knew that, whenever he recalled it in the future, the terrible finality of this winter afternoon would chill him to the bone.

An hour later Philip was riding hell for leather towards Coventry, on a borrowed horse. The ostler had given him some slurred instructions as to whom he should deliver it when he reached the fair, and he had wished Philip well.

On his back was a bag, stuffed with a change of clothes and a cold pigeon wrapped in cloth, the remains of dinner from the previous night. Apart from this he carried no possessions. He had left the house so quickly! His mother had kissed him farewell, and Philip had resisted her hugs and tears like a martyred soul. His father had said nothing.

CHAPTER THREE

Somewhere along the road, after riding for what seemed like hours, Philip slithered off his horse and tied it to a tree. He lay down under a hedge, shivering and crying. In the dark he ate the greasy cold pigeon, and it tasted of home, and this made Philip cry more. All around him he heard the creak and moan of trees, and the screams of foxes. After a while, he fell asleep.

The next morning he woke early, to the sound of voices. These were the other riders on the way to the fair.

'Wake up lad!'

Philip crawled out from under the hedge. His hair

was dirty and matted, his clothes damp. His horse, excited by the presence of other horses, was dragging on its tether, and stamping its hooves. Philip pulled his rucksack on to his back and scrambled on to the horse. He rode with the four other riders to Coventry. They were fifteen miles from the city.

The streets of Coventry were full of people – people leading strings of horses, selling oranges, asses' milk and roast chestnuts; gypsy wives in mink coats; people telling fortunes, haggling over ponies; little boys selling puppies. Philip was dazzled by the sun that shone on the people's gold rings and bracelets, on the gold and pink china for sale by the side of the road, and on the pavements wet with oil and water.

He followed the crowds to the centre of town and, obeying the ostler's instructions, handed over his horse to a dealer who had an ugly, crooked eye. He realised as he did this that he now had no way of getting home, and the feeling of fear and sickness filled his chest. For a while Philip wandered about in the crowds. He remembered his father's words – *what will you do*? He bit his lip and his eyes burned and flashed. Damn his father. Damn him. He would find something – anything – but he would not creep home like a lost dog. He would find his own way in the world.

At that moment he saw a man in a uniform with colourful ribbons in his cap. He was a recruiting sergeant, on the lookout for talented riders and brave men. In a loud voice and with a flourish of drums he announced:

'Here's General Elliott, Aide-de-Camp to His Majesty King George II, come to enlist you in his new regiment, the 15th Light Dragoons. Let powdered hair, drums and colours speak for themselves, and if you have a mind to wet your whistles with His Majesty's double beer, follow me.'

Philip Astley was hungry and penniless. He followed the recruiting officer, and asked him if he could help with the horses. The officer stared at his filthy face, and damp, bedraggled clothes. 'Not a penny to his name,' he thought to himself, 'probably a runaway of some sort.' But he saw that Philip was young, stubborn and fearless. He enlisted him on the spot as a groom. Now all Philip had to do was prove himself.

The army suited Philip. He grew tall and strong – with nerves of iron. He worked his way quickly up the ranks and it wasn't long before he was made an officer. He was a dashing sight in his scarlet uniform jacket with blue cuffs and white breeches. And he made many friends. He was adored by girls, who would gather to watch his daring riding in the sandy outdoor pen at the military headquarters. The other soldiers nicknamed him 'Hercules'.

In 1759 England was in the middle of the Seven Years War, which had begun three years earlier. This was a war about territory, with everyone confused and swapping sides. Most of the time Britain was fighting against France, Spain and Prussia (now part of Germany). To his relief Philip was ordered abroad on active service. He was inspired by the leadership of the King, George II, who was a brave man and an active soldier. He was the last monarch to fight alongside his men on the battlefield.

Philip was sent to war on a huge boat filled with soldiers, horses and a farmyard of animals for provisions – ducks, pigs, chickens and cows. He was put in charge of loading the frontline horses – they were the fastest, flightiest horses of all. Only Philip was trusted to organise these valuable steeds.

One day, when they were unloading in Hamburg, a black mare, startled by a loose chicken that flapped up out of the bottom of the ship, reared up and fell backwards off the edge of the gangplank into the cold water. Philip cursed the stupid chicken-handlers. They were always drunk. And now his best mare would be drowned in the currents. Without hesitation he pulled off his tunic and dived into the freezing water. He swam after the struggling horse, caught the rope of

her head-collar, and pulled her away from the boat and towards the shore, to safety. The men cheered from the quayside.

A year later, while the British were fighting alongside the Prussians and against the French at the Battle of Emsdorf, Philip showed again that he was made of heroic stuff. The Duke of Brunswick had charged into the enemy lines at the head of his troop of Prussian men, but had then fallen from his horse and was lying on the ground, surrounded by French soldiers. Undaunted, Philip rode to the rescue. Storming through the enemy lines, he drew near the injured man and, bending low from his horse, hooked one arm beneath the Duke to lift him from the ground, before seizing the enemy standard.

Philip, who doubted himself every day, thought little of his achievments – he was just fulfilling his promise to himself that he would be able to make it in the world on his own. But, despite this lack of self-confidence, he was making quite a name for himself. He was becoming famous throughout the army for his bravery and gusto. Not long after the Battle of Emsdorf, Philip was promoted to Sergeant Major and, on his regiment's triumphant return to London at the end of the Seven Years War, he was presented to the new King, George III.

The slightly bewildered Philip was patted on the back, saluted and cheered, and given a glass of a rich port. The powdered and wigged spokesman for the King announced that Philip was to be granted immediate discharge. Then, to Philip's utter astonishment, the King's men presented him with a beautiful white horse. He named the horse Gibraltar.

CHAPTER FOUR

When Sergeant-Major Philip Astley settled in London in the early 1760s, he had few possessions. All he owned was his scarlet uniform, a record of his adventures in the army and his beloved horse Gibraltar. He had some savings, but nothing else: he needed nothing else. Philip Astley's fortune lay in his ideas.

He felt relieved to be free from the army. Although a grown man, he was still as restless as a boy and the colour and life of London appealed to him. A proud man on a beautiful white horse – he would show his father what he could do!

London in the mid-18th century was a hectic, ever-changing place. The capital was being turned around, renewed and rebuilt. A bridge was erected between Westminster and Lambeth, to ease the congestion on London Bridge. The old gates around the City were demolished, and people with money began moving away from its narrow, dirt-ridden streets to build new houses in the fashionable West End. Everywhere the streets were being paved, and the chaotic old signs that used to hang outside people's houses were replaced with numbers.

People did not stand idle, hang about or defer to their masters as they had done in the old days. Throughout the city there was a brimming energy, a desire to get on and get out and be seen. Philip loved this new London. He loved the theatre of life that was being played out on the streets – the showing off and the exhibitionism of the new wealth. He loved the kaleidoscope of colour behind which people could hide their real selves.

And yet, beneath the colourful façade, these were cruel and chaotic times. Live chickens were stoned to death in the streets for sport, young children were burnt while sweeping thick soot from chimneys, miserable stray dogs were caged in the middle of Tottenham Court Road, and criminals were hanged at Tyburn (close to what is now Marble Arch). Unless you were one of the few to be born into wealth, and managed to survive both disease and the terrible remedies of disease, your life was destined to be short, brutish and miserable.

The people of London needed entertaining. These days we watch action films and play computer games with cars and guns and fights. In 18th-century London people got their thrills by watching trick-riders performing incredible stunts on horseback.

This was an age when nearly everyone could ride a horse if they needed to, but few could do so in the new and daring fashion of the trick-riders. A tight-knit bunch, glamorous and skilled, these men could ride their horses backwards, forwards, and stand in the saddle at a gallop; they could play instruments, fall off, and then leap back on again. The girls adored them; the men envied them; everyone wanted to be close to them. They were like pop stars and footballers rolled into one.

Trick-riding was the craze of the Regency age. The Industrial Revolution was just about to begin, and people were becoming more and more interested in trying to conquer the forces of nature. Dancing a jig while riding a horse seemed like splendid proof of man's ability to tame the wild.

Furthermore the theatre, where people used to meet, talk and be entertained, had lost its appeal. In 1737 the government had passed an act which closed down smaller theatres, and ordered that every play or show be approved by the authorities. As a result, of course, the theatre became no fun at all.

Trick-riding, on the other hand, with its promise of danger and rule-breaking, was a craze which would spread throughout the world. And the best place to see it was London, more specifically the Three Hats Inn, in Islington, where the landlord, Mr Dingly, had completely cornered the market. Every trick-rider worth his or her salt played at the Three Hats. And anyone lucky enough to get the chance to perform there was sure to become a star. Competition to work for Mr Dingly was very fierce indeed.

Philip heard all about the Three Hats in his first few weeks in London. He was loathe to just turn up and ask for a job – but he had nowhere else to go. He didn't want a normal job. He knew he was a good horseman, and deep down he also knew he was something of a show-off. There was no question about it: the glamorous, dark world of trick-riding was his destiny.

For his audition, Philip rode Gibraltar in the outdoor ring. He had learnt to trick-ride in the army, and he found it easy. He leapt on and off his white horse, stood on his hands, and danced a sort of Cossack dance. The horse's hooves pounded and churned the earth, sunlight shone brightly through the rising dustclouds – Philip was a more impressive sight than even he realised.

He was watched admiringly by Mr Dingly, a short fellow with a red face and watery eyes, and by two famous trick-riders: the handsome Thomas Johnson, who rode his horse naked, surrounded by bees which he had trained to swarm about him by smearing honey all over his body; and Mr Coningham, who played a flute whilst riding two horses, dressed as Cupid with his tiny son on his shoulders, firing gold arrows. He was also watched by Charles Hughes, Mr Coningham's assistant, who stared at Philip with jealousy and hatred in his blue eyes.

'You can ride, my lad, no doubt about that,' said Mr Dingly approvingly. 'You can start tomorrow. I'll see to it that someone finds you a room.'

Soon Philip was performing at the Three Hats Inn

every afternoon, attracting a huge crowd every day. He was also put in charge of the stables, having to make sure that all the horses were kept fit and well groomed.

As the months passed, and Philip's popularity grew, some of his less successful peers at the Three Hats began to resent him. Charles Hughes, whenever possible, tried to play tricks on him and to cause him trouble. But Philip, who barely had time to wash his hands and straighten his collar before going back out on stage, didn't even notice.

CHAPTER FIVE

Philip became a favourite of Mr Dingly's, and on occasion the two would sit up in the evening talking about work. One evening the subject turned to girls. Philip didn't really have time for a girlfriend – he was too busy proving himself to the world. But there were times, when, still missing home, he felt extremely lonely.

'There's one girl, Mr Dingly, who's caught my eye. I was just about to do that trick, you know, where I jump from Gibraltar and then cross the ring and jump back on him without breaking from a gallop... Gibraltar is the finest horse in London, Mr Dingly, don't forget.'

Mr Dingly nodded and smiled, his eyes watering a little.

'This girl', Philip continued, 'the blonde girl with the red roses in her hair, she caught my eye, and though, of course, I didn't miss the trick, I couldn't stop thinking about her. It was as if I did the act just for her. After the show I wanted to go out the front and meet her, but had to help Charles with something – one of his horses actually got loose – so I couldn't. She hasn't been back since, has she? You don't know where can I find her, do you?'

Mr Dingly said nothing, and changed the subject. But he was worried. He had seen the drama played out so many times before. A great rider, a splendid horse, and an admiring lady. It was a terrible combination – and in this case he might lose his best act. After that evening he made sure that Philip was too occupied backstage to spend time chatting up girls.

But nothing could make Philip forget the blonde beauty. He became more and more restless, until eventually he felt unhappy in his work. One day, while sweeping the cobbled yard by the stables, he confided in Charles Hughes that he might soon leave Mr Dingly's establishment, and look for work elsewhere. He wanted to be free to find the girl who had stolen his heart. She haunted his every waking moment – on the brief occasions when he was free to walk or ride through the city he would imagine he saw her, walking across Westminster Bridge, or stepping from a sedan chair on to the pavement outside Covent Garden. Charles was all ears, and that evening he bought Philip a pint to cheer him up.

But, though he might have seemed to be a good friend to Philip, Hughes was anything but – he was jealous and spiteful, and he wanted Philip sacked. The next day he sneaked off to Mr Dingly and blurted out that Philip would soon be leaving the Three Hats Inn.

What a row this news would create! Mr Dingly would be sure to sack Philip at once for disloyalty. Charles Hughes congratulated himself on his cunning plan. Soon, he hoped, he would see the back of Philip

Astley, and the yard of the Three Hats Inn horses would be his again.

But it was not the case. Mr Dingly did not want to lose his protégé. 'If Philip needs the company of girls,' Mr Dingly thought to himself, 'then I shall have to employ girls.' He knew it was the only sure way to keep the young lad from leaving for good.

A few days later Mr Dingly gathered together all his riders and told them that he was expecting a female rider to join the troupe. Philip was surprised. Few women were attracted to the dangerous art of trick-riding. It was glamorous to watch, but actually doing it was a tough business – broken legs, smashed noses, hands worn and cracked, the company of rough men and wild horses. Who on earth had Dingly found who was willing to take on such a life?

'You are to find for her a horse with perfect manners,' Mr Dingly told Philip, ' I have a feeling that this girl will prove to be most popular with the gentlemen. She is daring and skilled, but at the same time, graceful, like a swan – she is quite unique.'

Sugar Rawlinson had blond hair to the waist and a tiny, yet perfect, physique. Her smile sparkled like ice. Her arrival at the Three Hats sent a ripple of excitement through the establishment, and, like all newcomers, she rode on her first morning in the out-door ring watched by all the other riders.

Philip was the last to arrive, and as he walked over to the assembled group – Dingly, Charles Hughes and Mr Johnson – he saw that the beautiful girl riding around the ring, singing and dancing like a doll on the back of Dingly's favourite horse, was none other than the girl who had so bewitched him all those weeks ago.

'Can this be true, Dingly – how did you find her?'

Mr Dingly looked confused.

'What do you mean Philip?'

'That's her, that's the girl I was telling you about!'

Mr Dingly's delight in his new recruit now turned rapidly to dismay. This was not what he had planned at all; it seemed that he had booked the very girl who might take his prize rider away.

After the excitement of Sugar's arrival, everyone at the Three Hats Inn settled back into the familiar routine of shows and work. Sugar and Philip became close friends. Skilled, charismatic and ambitious, they were a mirror to each other's dreams. Sugar was obsessive about her work: she would exercise constantly, never eat more than a mouthful or two, and she got up at dawn to practise every single day. She drew diagrams of all the trick-riding movements in a little blue notebook. She was fastidious about the fitting of her horse's harness; soon she would trust only Philip to do it. It was not long before they fell in love.

Meanwhile, Charles Hughes was boiling over with jealousy. Philip – tall, dark-haired and handsome – was still the star, still loved by Dingly, and now he was effortlessly winning the heart of the most dazzling girl in London. Hughes lurked in their shadow, wishing evil on them, longing for them to leave the Three Hats and work somewhere else. Little did he realise how soon his dreams would be answered.

Before long, the young couple announced that they were going to be married. Romantic though it was, this turned out to be a shrewd business move. For Philip and Sugar had a powerful aura about them whenever they were together. As a performing duo, they were an unbeatable combination. And they knew it... It was time to break away from Mr Dingly.

Poor Mr Dingly was devastated when Philip told him his news. The Three Hats would suffer terribly from the loss. But he knew there was no stopping Philip when he had made up his mind.

Hughes, on the other hand, was delighted. As he said goodbye to the happy couple, he wished them good luck, while in his heart he cursed them and prayed that they might fail in everything they did.

CHAPTER SIX

Philip and Sugar were married in a church in Holborn. The following morning they walked to Smithfield Market and bought two horses: a large riding horse which they called Isaac, and a small brown pony named Billy. They rented a house, just big enough for their few possessions and with its own stables, in a fashionable street between St James's Park and the River Thames. Mr Dingly and the Three Hats seemed a lifetime away.

Every day, full of new love and optimism, they rode across the new Westminster Bridge to the fields on the other side of the river, leaving the bustle of the city far behind them; Philip on Gibraltar, Sugar on Isaac leading little Billy. Philip loved the wide-open green space south of the river, and he decided to rent some land there. He found a spot in Lambeth Fields at a place called Half Penny Hatch, so called after the halfpenny toll that was charged on all those who walked over the bridge which crossed the stream that ran alongside the field.

Philip and Sugar had set their hearts on re-inventing trick-riding. And, over the next six months, they used up all their savings to feed themselves and their three horses while they practised a new act. They thought of trick-riding as a brand new form of theatre, a new language for telling stories. From morning until night they worked together, conjuring up ideas for new and ever more thrilling exploits on horse-back.

The sight of Philip Astley and his beautiful young wife galloping around on their wild horses in the damp fields just south of the river attracted a varied crowd of spectators. Itinerant musicians, farmers on their way to market, groups of French paupers picking dandelions to sell at the inns around the city – they all stopped and stared. But Philip did not want anyone to see what they were doing before they were completely ready. He was nervous that their show would be copied, or that it might not even be good enough for the demanding public.

'And then, who am I?' he asked himself, 'a failed entertainer, a vagabond runaway who should have been a carpenter!' – and he was miserable and bit his lip. In the end, the passers-by made him so nervous that he built a high wooden wall around their practice ring, making a kind of open-air amphitheatre.

Safe from prying eyes, Philip and Sugar now practised as if their lives depended on it. And the truth was it did; they were so poor that their horses ate better than they did. The only help they got was from a young boy called Edward Foundling.

Edward was an orphan who had been found as a baby abandoned in the streets of the notorious slum area of St Giles. A small scrap of paper pinned to his shirt had read: 'Seduc'd and reduc'd.' Nothing else was known about him. He had been taken to the Foundling Hospital in Gray's Inn, and, aged six, had been sent out to work, to groom horses for a company that ran coaches from London to the provinces. It was at the London stables that Philip found him and offered to take him on as a stable boy. He could not have hoped for a more loyal friend.

**

Months went by and then, at last, Philip and Sugar felt ready to perform in public. The announcement of the grand opening of Astley's show caused a stir that rippled through the coffee houses and inns of the city. People remembered the glamorous trick-rider of the Three Hats, and they wanted more of his rough charm. They were also keen to see what had happened to Sugar Rawlinson, with her filmy silk dresses and glittering eyes.

On the morning of their first performance Philip was up early, so that he could stand on Westminster

Bridge and proclaim to the crowds: 'Grand opening of Astley's Amphitheatre! Today at one o'clock! The most daring tricks you will ever see.'

His voice carried on the wind, loud and strong. He was every inch the showman. But his stomach churned and he felt dizzy with fear. His fear was the fear of every impresario. What if no one comes? What if it is a disaster? He feared that he had made himself and his wife a laughing-stock. What if they made no money? What if they were ruined and had to find work as poor servants? Philip – bold and daring on horseback – feared failure more than anything in the world, more even than death.

CHAPTER SEVEN

BANG! Edward stands on a wooden pigeon coop at the centre of the ring, and with his drum announces that the show will start in half an hour.

One o'clock has struck and the amphitheatre is full. It is a sunny day and everyone is in a holiday mood. The crowds push through the doors. Philip spots the face of Charles Hughes in the audience, and he is touched that his old friend from the Three Hats Inn has come to support him. Charles Hughes catches Philip's eye and smiles and waves.

Bang! Into the ring rides Philip on Gibraltar, who gallops energetically around the edge.

He stands on one leg, and then jumps round in the

saddle to face Gibraltar's tail. The horse continues to gallop apace, while Philip, roaring like a lion, turns himself upside down in the saddle so that he balances on his head. With one hand holding on to the saddle, Philip draws his pistol and fires it. The noise of the shot ricochets around the small arena.

Bang! Isaac gallops into the ring. He draws up alongside Philip and Gibraltar. Philip puts one foot on to Isaac's saddle, one on to Gibraltar's, and in this daring fashion sails around the ring with his arms spread wide. He and the two horses then leap out of the wooden theatre, into a gap in the audience. The crowd's faces are filled with fear, and at the same time amazement.

Bang! Billy trots daintily into the ring. Philip enters the ring after him and calls Billy over. It is as if man and horse are talking to each other. The people are silent. Whereas before they had been excited and disturbed by the vision of man and horse galloping in such precarious unison, now they are hushed. Suspense prickles the hot air.

A drunk in the audience, intoxicated by gin, starts to shout, and the crowd pushes him roughly toward the door of the amphitheatre. Silence falls again.

Entering with enthusiasm into this change of mood, Edward effects a low drum roll, which Philip silences with a fierce look. Edward blushes red. All the focus must be on Billy. The little pony rolls over as if he were dead. To the audience he is dead.

Philip lifts and drops the pony's outstretched leg. No one stirs. Then with a flourish of brilliantly coloured silk handkerchiefs, he brings the dead pony back to life. First the pony sits, then he stands, and then, with the growing applause of the crowd, he rears right up on his hind legs and paws the air with his hooves.

Bang! In a swirl of cream silk, Sugar flies into the ring with Gibraltar and Isaac, a foot on each of the two horses.

She circles Philip and Billy, and with a shout and a laugh, her blue eyes glittering in the sun, she chases them from the ring. Her hair cascades in blonde

ringlets down her back, and her skirts fly with the speed of the galloping horses. In her hand she carries a pistol which she fires into the sky with such enthusiasm that everyone recoils before bursting into loud cheers and applause.

And now, the first drops of thundery rain begin to fall, drawing the performance to its natural end. Sugar comes to a halt in the centre of the ring. There is a film of sweat on her smiling face. Philip, sweating also, rides into the ring on Gibraltar, with little Billy following after.

Relieved that the show is a success, Philip rests for a moment as he stands with Gibraltar listening to the audience's claps and cheers and shouts. He glances at Sugar. He can see that she is thrilled too, and he leans forward and pats Gibraltar's damp neck.

'Good boy,' he murmurs.

But despite the triumph of the afternoon, Philip realises that this show is only a start. Now they will have to produce more shows, always coming up with new ideas and new tricks. For a second, he shudders:

Will he never be able to rest again?

As the audience cheers, Philip and Sugar do a lap of honour around the ring. The people leap to their feet, clapping more wildly and shouting for more.

CHAPTER EIGHT

Luckily for Philip the craze for trick-riding showed no signs of stopping. Throughout that summer Philip, Sugar, Edward and the horses played to packed houses in their little enclosed ring on the fields of Lambeth. At the height of the season they were taking forty guineas a day (worth about £3,500 in today's money). But still Philip went out early every morning to ride around the streets of the city on Gibraltar, drumming up business.

It was exhausting work – weaving between the carriages, avoiding the dead cats and ditches over-flowing with mud and rubbish. But it was essential to keep the public coming to their shows. Without an audience, a show ceases to exist.

Philip now began to realise that trick-riding alone would not satisfy the public. The rich daughters of grand families, the merchants, hotel keepers, horsemen, highwaymen, tourists, dandies, playboys, the old dames with bug-eyed lap dogs – they all wanted new and original things to see.

'Dancing ostriches, mind-reading hedgehogs, intelligent fleas, ponies that can add up and make the tea – what else can we serve up for the people?' asked Philip in his sleep, grinding his teeth. All day and all night he wondered what he had to do next, where he could find the next act. There were times when Sugar thought that he had almost forgotten about her.

Nevertheless, before long, and despite his distraction, Sugar gave birth to a beautiful blond-haired baby. She adored the wriggling little child, and lavished untold love on him. Philip loved the child too, but as autumn approached, and he knew the performing season was coming to a close, he fell into depression. The weather grew wet and cold, and people gradually drifted back to the theatres. It was time to do something else to earn the family some money.

With a heavy heart, he decided he would have to go on the road. He saddled up Gibraltar and, leaving Sugar and the the baby (whom they had named John), he joined the wandering trail of clowns, acrobats, animal-handlers and conjurors, medicine-men, rope dancers, contortionists and gypsies, who moved from fair to fair throughout the autumn months. He could raise money at these fairs, through horse-dealing and trick-riding. What's more, he calculated, he could see what else was out there, what else he could bring home for his show next summer.

'I have a beautiful wife and a delightful son,' he told himself. 'But they will still be here when I get home. They can manage without me for a while. If we rest, we will be ruined. I must press on – we have to be the best.'

***

Philip met many different performers and artistes. One man had a pair of deer and a ram that could count. He saw two lions as docile as dogs, rats that could walk the tightrope and dance to violins, cats that played the dulcimer and squalled in time to the notes, dancing turkeys, learned pigs, trained snakes, dancers, tumblers, jugglers and acrobats. He had a good memory for names and faces, and before long he had a whole address book of eccentric performers in his head.

But Philip also saw misery. Homelessness was a much bigger problem in the 18th century than it is today, and every big city swarmed with beggars and drunks. There was suffering everywhere: disease, poverty, theft, and murder never seemed far away.

Amid the hullabaloo, as the lanterns on the stalls were being lit and the gin bars were beginning to fill, Philip often thought of home. He knew that this was not the life for him or his son. He dreamt of finer things, of managing his own theatre, a place always filled with posh ladies and fine gentlemen. He desperately wanted to get out of the mud – to build himself a big house, and clothe his family in suits of silk and satin.

One evening in November, Philip and Gibraltar were camped in a quiet lane, somewhere between Cheltenham and Oxford. Dark figures crept up on them during the night and Philip woke to discover that they were trying to steal his horse. Luckily he had got into the habit of sleeping with a metal bar beside him, just in case he needed to protect himself. In a second he grasped hold of the bar and jumped to his feet. Stepping between the men and his horse, he caught the first one hard across the shoulders. When the second came forward shouting and waving his fists, Philip hit him across the head.

Terrified by Philip's strength and gargantuan size, the thieves ran away. But Philip was badly shaken, and he left immediately, riding through the darkness for five hours, not stopping until daybreak.

He and his horse had escaped unhurt, but the episode depressed him. He was Sergeant-Major Philip

Astley, hero of the 15th Light Dragoons. He had come a long way since running away from home aged sixteen. He lived in a decent furnished house. He had a baby who was free from disease and a wife who could afford to buy new dresses. Yet here he was out on the road fighting for a living. He knew how to survive. But that wasn't enough for him anymore; he wanted security. That night he made up his mind to return to London and buy some property. He remembered his father's anger when he had left home; this insecure, itinerant life was exactly what old Edward had tried to warn him about.

The road back to London was clogged with mud. It was November and the days were short and cold. Along the way Philip met other artists, all heading to London for work. Many, like him, had a family to support. Over a watery beer at an alehouse in Banbury, he met an Italian tightrope dancer whose act involved balancing on a rope with a wheelbarrow containing his two children and a dog. He could even sing a song at the same time. The Italian, in a mixture of broken English and theatrical gestures, explained to Philip that he wanted to work in a theatre. He, like so many wandering players, was worn out by the uncertainty of life on the road.

A plan was forming in Philip's mind. He would own a theatre that would stage not just acrobatics on horseback, but also dramas, dances and musicals, with a cast of characters straight out of a fairytale. He sensed that the popularity of trick-riding alone might soon wane, and he imagined a vast glittering amphitheatre, with a glass roof lit by hundreds and thousands of jets of light, full of the most magnificent horses in London, and frequented by kings and queens. As he rode closer to London, these ideas grew in his mind, and he felt the familiar churning in his stomach as he realised that he had a huge task ahead of him.

***

Philip was on the last leg of his long journey when he

was joined by someone else on horseback. At first Philip did not recognise the rider, in his thick cloak and dark hat. Then, as the horse drew near, he realised that it was his old friend Charles Hughes.

'Charles! How are you? What are you doing these days?'

'Like you Philip, I have been out on the road at the fairs, breaking horses for the gentry, doing the odd deal. There is plenty out here to keep people entertained, eh Philip? We could learn a lot from all these new acts and ideas, don't you think?'

Philip looked at Charles's smiling face, half hidden by the shadow cast by his hat. He had caught something in Charles's tone of voice that instantly made him regret his spontaneous friendliness. Charles looked thin and drawn, older somehow and meaner.

'But it's hard, isn't it, Philip, the life out here?' Charles went on. 'The constant moving, the fight for every last shilling some passer-by might throw. And in your case, surely, there's no need for it anymore... You had quite a summer of it back in

London. You and Sugar have been doing well, very well... I have been watching you, Philip.'

Philip felt deeply uneasy now. Yes, life at the fairs was no picnic, but Charles's tone of voice was sarcastic, almost threatening. For a split second he remembered the dark figures who had attacked him in the night. He was tired and worn out by the long ride back to London, and a flicker of suspicion passed over his mind. Could Charles have had something to do with the assault? Could he really have been reduced to that?

Then, ashamed of himself, Philip banished such slanderous thoughts. Surely, Charles Hughes meant him no harm. He was a familiar face in a friendless world, and he was pleased to ride with him the rest of the way to London.

CHAPTER NINE

Philip was overjoyed to see Sugar and baby John again, but he was distracted. His heart was set on owning a theatre of his own; and within a few weeks of his return he managed to raise enough money to buy an old timberyard by Westminster Bridge, away from the jostle of Lambeth fields and closer to the gentrified heart of the capital.

Here he planned to build a proper amphitheatre, with covered seats and elegant decorations. Philip had a few savings, he had an investment in a new saddler's shop that was doing well, and he had also incurred an extraordinary stroke of good luck. One day, crossing Westminster Bridge on his return home, he had seen something glinting in the dirt on the road in front of him. A gold ring! Philip had picked the ring up, sold it, and used the proceeds to start the building work.

He wanted his new show to be different from anything he, or anyone else, had ever seen. Stories would be told in plays, music, songs, dancing and acrobatics. There would be staged mock battles where the contestants would fight with blackened sticks; he'd get the Italian tightrope dancer he had met on the road, and a group of dancing dogs. Most importantly of all, they would be able to put shows on all the year round. He was determined that they would be grander and more impressive than anything ever seen before.

The theatre scene at that time was having to adjust to the newly established popularity of the trick-riders. In 1737 King George II had decreed that no establishment as ordinary as the Three Hats Inn could include speaking actors in its shows; this privilege was to be reserved for the great theatres of Covent Garden and Drury Lane. But Philip and the other outlaw showmen thought up ways round this. Horses, they decreed, would become actors (*hippodrama*) and dialogue would be set to music (*burlesque*).

Nothing was going to stop the Astleys. 'Everything we have worked towards is going to happen now!' Philip told Sugar. He assumed, of course, that his wife would be as happy as he was. The mud and the rough fields at Lambeth could now become part of family folklore, nothing more than a fond memory of past struggles.

But Sugar did not smile. The glitter was gone from her eyes and she looked at Philip as if she didn't trust him.

'What's the matter?' he asked.

'Philip, don't you know?' she exclaimed. 'You must have heard what people have been saying. You have been accused of terrible crimes – of robbery and... blackmail!'

'No-one knows,' she continued, 'how you raised the money for the amphitheatre. Even I don't know. You told me about the ring, but it does sound a bit far-fetched, doesn't it? Everyone is talking about us, but now for the wrong reasons. Everywhere I go people look at me with distrust – as if a shadow is hanging about me like an old woman's cloak.'

Philip had also heard the rumours, and he too was beginning to feel a little worried. At his lowest moments he couldn't help but think back to his encounter with Charles Hughes, whose strange words still rang in his ears: '*I've been watching you Philip...*'

But he banished such suspicions from his mind. He didn't want to dwell on dark thoughts. He knew what he had to do to clear his name, and without wasting any more time he sent Edward off to Islington to announce to Mr Dingly that he and Gibraltar would appear the next day at the Three Hats to give a brief, impromptu performance.

And so it was that on a damp afternoon in early 1770 Philip found himself back at Mr Dingly's in Islington, riding in the enclosure where he had first performed before the public. He knew the crowd there was on tenterhooks, wondering why he had returned and whether the rumours about him were true.

That afternoon Philip gave a brilliant performance, as was expected of him by the public. At the end of the act he jumped from Gibraltar, handed the reins to Edward Foundling, and turned to address his audience. It seemed to Philip that for a moment the cacophony of the city was silenced. A damp fog was descending and the air was still and heavy. The musicians dropped their instruments, the street urchins stopped screaming, the lapdogs stopped yapping. All was silent as Philip spoke.

'Hear me now, oh people of London! This is a true and honest tale, the tale of how I, Sergeant-Major Philip Astley, came to build a smart new amphitheatre beside the River Thames. Now, while walking across Westminster Bridge on a fine morning some weeks ago, I happened to see, lying on the ground, almost concealed between two granite paving slabs, a diamond ring. I took it to the magistrate, and waited for it to be claimed by the unfortunate individual who had dropped it. This individual did not appear, so the ring remained uncollected. The law says that an article lost after thirty days "shall be returned to the person or persons who retrieved the said article" [Philip had spent some time researching this subject and could remember legal phrases as if they were songs], 'and so, I collected the ring and sold it. And I intend to use the proceeds to build the finest riding hall in London!'

The crowd let out an uproarous cheer. Philip waited for the noise to die down before going on.

'I invite you all to come to Astley's Amphitheatre when it's open, and I promise...' – he paused for dramatic effect – '...I promise you... you won't be disappointed!'

Philip turned on his heels and walked out. He was pleased with his performance, but even now he felt defeated and empty. There were many people who still would not believe him, and what's more Mr Dingly was furious that he had so brazenly advertised his own show in the ring at the Three Hats. It seemed to Philip that whatever he did now he made enemies, and that the more famous he was, the more people hated him and wanted him to fail.

'Still,' he said to Edward, as they saddled up their horses to go home, 'the job is done. People can say what they like, Edward. It won't stop our plans.'

Just as they were about to leave the yard, a man appeared out of the shadows. Charles Hughes.

'I heard your little speech in there Philip,' said Charles with a twist in his grin. 'But people will never believe the likes of you and me, will they, friend? Riders, showmen, gypsies – we are all one and the same in their eyes. But I've been thinking Philip. Two is always stronger than one. Yes, I've been thinking... perhaps we should join forces one day?'

Charles' words made Philip feel uncomfortable, but he was tired and didn't want to say anything which might cause offence, or lead to a row. Inclining his head slightly, he bade Charles goodnight, promising to show him round the Amphitheatre when it was finished. Philip and Edward then got on their horses and set off home through the thick London fog.

CHAPTER TEN

When Astley's Amphitheatre was at last ready to open, at the start of the summer season on Easter Monday 1770, the house was packed. Philip had forgotten about the mean rumours, Sugar had forgiven him, and they were doing what they did best – pulling crowds and entertaining people. Their ingenious combination of trick-riding and other acts was an immediate hit. Philip and Sugar, without even knowing it, had invented the circus.

The art of circus means taking lots of different people and ideas, and putting them together to create a new and original show, which is no easy task. But Philip had a gift; he was a supreme showman, bringing together acts of a dazzling variety. Not just trick-riding but acrobatics, swordsmanship, comic turns, songs and dancing. Whatever Philip was doing intrigued people. His work had all the glamour and razzle-dazzle needed to bring in the crowds. Every day his father's words were in his mind, and every day he felt he had to prove himself to the world once again.

For the new amphitheatre he recruited a large troupe of the finest trick-riders – performers such as the Vangable family, who had the balancing skill of cats and the agility of monkeys. Mr and Mrs Vangable walked on their toes and pointed their noses in the air. They wore a different pair of shoes every day of the week, and always wore yellow gloves for any sort of rough work. They never drank alcohol, and were fastidious about washing. Even their daughter, who was only nine years old, was a better trick-rider than Philip. She was billed as the youngest rider in London.

And then, one morning, Philip was paid a visit by Mr Charles Hughes. Philip was surprised and pleased to learn that Charles had got married. His wife's name was Veronica. She was the genteel daughter of a shipping insurer. Philip thought her quite charming; she had a beautiful gleaming smile which showed off her unusually white teeth, unmarked by pyorrhoea or scurvy (she brushed her teeth every night with a new bristle brush, and the one tooth she had lost she had replaced with a piece of walrus tooth). But underneath that smile, unbeknownst to Philip, she was mercenary. Her heart was as cold as stone.

Charles asked Philip if he and Veronica could join Philip's troupe; he had fallen out with Dingly and confided in Philip that the Three Hats was going to wrack and ruin. Although Philip didn't entirely trust Charles, he agreed. Of course he would help his old friend. Why, only a short time ago he himself had been in the same position, newly married and without a home.

With the Hughes family on board, Astley's Amphitheatre was busier than ever. Sugar, increasingly taken up with the demands of bringing up baby

John, didn't have much time to pander to her husband in the way she had done, which meant that Philip found himself paying more and more attention to Veronica. Indeed, generous as he was, he taught Charles and Veronica all he knew, instructing them both in the finer points of trick-riding. He helped with costume ideas, with selecting just the right horse, and with all their rehearsals.

By the end of a year's engagement with the Astleys, Veronica had developed her own tricks, and was a popular feature of the show. And it was then that Philip began to see through her superficial smiles. He could not help noticing that the many compliments she and Charles received for the brilliance of their act were gracefully accepted, and yet neither of them ever acknowledged Philip and all that he had taught them.

Soon into the second year of their contract with him, Veronica and Charles announced that they were leaving. Philip wasn't surprised. They had got what they needed from Astley's Amphitheatre; in fact, in many ways it was a relief: he was pleased to see the back of them.

But a few months later Philip was in the stables looking after a mare and her newly born foal when Edward appeared at the end of the row of stalls. He seemed upset. Philip stood up and stared at Edward's anxious face. Edward was *never* worried, or upset. He had grown into a man who was hardly ever surprised; he usually took even serious matters as a joke.

'What on earth is the matter, Ed?'

'That Charles Hughes, he's only gone and built his own amphitheatre, sir, on that piece of land at Blackfriars Bridge. All that building work that we thought was going to be houses; well that's him. And it's just like ours and it opens this week. Everyone is talking about it! Everyone! He has got acts younger than Miss Vangable. He's got more horses than us! He's got all his acts out now, as we speak, parading up and down Westminster!'

Philip felt dizzy with fury. So he had been right all along. He should never have trusted the scoundrel Hughes.

Philip marched into the yard. He instructed every member of his company to saddle all the riding horses and harness up the driving horses. The clowns must be in costume. The Vangables were called from their room. As they began to complain that this was not in their contract, Philip silenced them with a scowl.

Within an hour, Philip, mounted on Gibraltar, leading Bill by his side, with his musicians and jugglers following on, was processing through Westminster calling out that Charles Hughes was an impostor, and that he, Philip Astley, was proprietor of the only true riding-house in London.

Though he appeared angry, Philip was actually deeply pained. He had trusted Charles and Veronica Hughes. He had taught them everything he knew, paid them well for the privilege – and they had utterly betrayed him. The lovely Veronica had made a fool of him. Using his horses, and the skills that he had taught her, she had created an act that was now being billed in direct competition with his own. Philip's heart hardened; his trust in people had gone.

***

As for the public, they found this open war between two brilliant showman highly entertaining. And war it was. When Philip presented a nine-year-old rider who could vault from a cantering horse, Hughes presented an eight-year-old rider who could vault from a galloping horse. If Philip rode with a pint-pot balanced on his head, then sure as eggs were eggs, a week later Hughes would produce a rider who could gallop with a whole stack of pots on his head.

For the first time in his life, it seemed that Philip was losing his touch. A head-to-head battle is never a good backdrop for creative work. As the months went on, his show became less popular, and his performers started to look around for other positions. No one wants to work for a man on the way down. And Philip these days seemed to be more concerned with how he might avenge himself on those vile Hugheses than how would keep his circus supreme. Only a miracle could save him...

CHAPTER ELEVEN

Sergeant-Major Philip Astley was a man who made his own luck and fortune. And, in fact, it was not a miracle that was to save him, but his own imagination and will to succeed. It was sink or swim in the lusty world of 18th-century show-business, and Astley was determined to swim. Charles's betrayal had forced him to grow from a runaway boy, throwing all his heart at the world, into a calculating business man. He saw the circus as belonging to him. He had invented it. And so, he reasoned, the right to profit from the dazzling spectacle of horses and human performers was his alone.

He would do whatever it took to bring the public

back to him. He would put on shows not just through the summer, but all the year round. The amphitheatre was magnificent in every detail: the glass roof was painted with leaves and branches to look like an enchanted forest and the lighting glittered like a handful of jewels. All this finery cost so much money that Sugar was terrified that they would go bankrupt.

But as time went by some strange manic force seemed to take a hold of Philip's mind. He became more obsessed than ever before about thinking up new ideas to draw in the crowds. One of his new tricks even involved indoor fireworks (don't try this at home!); every evening he would ride into the ring on Gibraltar letting off Roman candles and small handheld fireworks that fell and crackled about him like golden rain.

In March 1784 he organised the first ever ascent of a hot-air balloon in England, on St George's fields, not far from his amphitheatre. The balloon, which was launched at about half past one in the afternoon, was later found at Faversham in Kent. The event caused so much excitement that for months afterwards every souvenir shop in London sold nick-nacks in the shape of little hot-air balloons.

Philip was gratified and proud.

'Sugar,' he declared the next day, 'that crowd was without doubt the greatest crowd ever to have assembled in the history of crowds!'

Sugar smiled. She had grown used to her husband's hyperbole. 'And what's more, Philip,' she replied, 'we have a new star in the making.'

'Who?' he asked.

'Our son John of course,' She replied, laughing. 'He is going to be the talk of the town soon.'

John had grown up in a family dedicated to horses and trick-riding. And Philip had always been determined that his son should join the family business. It had never occurred to him that this was the very same pressure against which he himself had rebelled all those years ago.

But John was no rebel. Delicate and fussy, he was encouraged by his mother to be the perfect little gentleman. When he watched the other children around him – the son of one of Philip's riders, for instance, was beaten by his father when he fell from a horse and broke his leg – John was thankful that his parents were not so tough with him. He had the best of everything: dance teachers, riding instructers, and even choreographers who helped him at every stage. He had no idea of his father's terrible struggles, or of the pain that drove him to succeed. Little John simply took it for granted that he was heir to the famous amphitheatre, and that he would one day be the star of the show.

And sure enough, he was soon to be seen in every performance, and the public loved him. He learnt to dance minuets and play the hornpipe on horseback. It was boasted that he was better than the famous Parisian dancer, Gaetano Vestris. The amazing Astley family were becoming living legends – circus idols.

They were often written about in the popular press. When the cynical writer Horace Walpole went to watch the show because he 'could find nothing else to do' on a dreary afternoon in March, he came away utterly astounded and wrote a long newspaper article telling everyone how simply unbelievable the show really was.

Here is one of the programmes for Astley's Amphitheatre in 1788, with John, who was known as 'Young Astley', as the star. He was eighteen years old:

YOUNG ASTLEY'S
SURPRISING EQUESTRIAN EXERCISES

✳

IN THE INTERVALS

✳

A NEW WAR ENTERTAINMENT

✳

IN WHICH WILL BE INTRODUCED A SINGLE COMBAT
WITH THE BROADSWORD BETWEEN YOUNG ASTLEY, AS
A BRITISH SAILOR, AND MR J. TAYLOR AS A SAVAGE
CHIEF; AFTER WHICH A GENERAL ENGAGEMENT
BETWEEN BRITISH SAILORS AND SAVAGES...

TUMBLING

BY A MOST CAPITAL GROUP...

✳

A MUSICAL ENTERTAINMENT,

CALLED THE INVITATION...

A GRAND ENTRY OF HORSES

A MINUET DANCE BY TWO HORSES

AND OTHER EXTRAORDINARY

PERFORMANCES BY THE HORSES

✳

A NEW COMIC DANCE, CALLED

THE ETHIOPIAN FESTIVAL...

✳

A NEW FAVOURITE SONG ...

CALLED BOW-WOW-WOW.

✳

HORSEMANSHIP...

BY MASTER CROSSMAN, MR JENKINS,

MR LONSDALE, MR J. TAYLOR

AND MISS VANGABLE...

THE WHOLE TO CONCLUDE WITH A NEW

ENTERTAINMENT OF SINGING, DANCING AND DUMB-
SHEW TO SPEAKING MUSIC, CALLED THE MAGIC
WORLD. IN WHICH WILL BE INTRODUCED, BEHIND
A LARGE TRANSPARENT PAINTING,
REPRESENTING THE ENCHANTED WORLD, A
VARIETY OF MAGICAL, PANTOMIMICAL, FARCICAL,
TRAGICAL, COMIC DECEPTIONS, TOGETHER WITH
A GRAND PROCESSION OF CARICATURE FIGURES,
DISPLAYING A VARIETY OF WHIMSICAL DEVICES
IN A MANNER ENTIRELY NEW.

✳

DOORS TO BE OPENED AT HALF-PAST FIVE,
AND TO BEGIN PRECISELY AT HALF-PAST SIX.

✳

BOXES 3 SHILLINGS

PIT 2 SHILLINGS

GALLERY 1 SHILLING

SIDE GALLERY 6 PENCE

George III was so impressed by the new acts that he granted Philip a fourteen-year patent for his methods of horse-breaking, and invited him to give a special royal show in Richmond gardens. Philip used the proceeds to build a huge house for himself and his family, which he decided to call Hercules Hall, in celebration of his own indomitable strength.

CHAPTER TWELVE

In the early 1780s Philip Astley took his troupe on a grand tour of Europe. John, Sugar, Philip and their entourage of artistes and helpers felt like one huge family on a camping trip; they were all excited to be away from London and the gossip merchants. The horses were shipped to Dover, and from there the Astley circus set off on a year-long gallivant that would take them from Brussels to Vienna, and even as far as Belgrade.

On the way back to London, the troupe visited the beautiful city of Paris. They met lots of important people there, including even certain members of the French royal family. And to everyone's astonishment, the Queen herself, Marie Antoinette, fell hopelessly in love with John, and didn't even try to make a secret of the fact. She swooned over his gentlemanly English manner, his soft blond hair and his extraordinary equestrian dancing. A handsome man in command of a fine horse – what more could a queen ask for? Her pulse would race uncontrollably every time she saw him.

This was the beginning of a short love affair between the French royal family and the English circus family. Indeed, the French Queen was so enthusiastic about the Astley family and their circus that she commissioned them to create an amphitheatre for her in the grounds of the royal palace.

When the troupe returned to London, John stayed on in Paris to run the new 'royal' amphitheatre. But John was a feckless fellow, and soon found someone else to do most of the work, so that he could be free to spend most of his time enjoying himself and entertaining Marie Antoinette. They spent many an afternoon lolling in comfortable chairs, swapping gossip and discussing fashion and wigs and make-up.

Philip saw his son enjoying a glamorous life in high society, and he reflected on the struggles of his own hard upbringing. Still, he didn't begrudge John anything – and he knew that royal favour could only help his own reputation. He understood that as long as he could hold on to the approval of the gentry, and provide an endless string of new amusements, his enterprises would not fall from favour.

But, though he had become more cynical with his years and experience, Philip still believed in the essential fairness of life. He still believed that with hard work and shrewd thinking he could make anything successful, and that people like Charles Hughes, who stole success from others, would always be sure to fail in the end.

And he was right. As the years passed, Charles Hughes's establishment became little more than a drinking saloon, while Philip's amphitheatre by Westminster Bridge was given royal approval, and renamed Royal Grove.

Desperate to keep up with the latest fashions, Philip found all kinds of things to draw in the crowds; he even managed to find a boy who could talk to pigeons and an Indian snake-charmer. But in his endless quest for financial security he also invested in a few of the small, more respectable businesses which had sprung up around the amphitheatre, like printing houses and saddleries. He also gave benefit performances, and did charitable works. For, as Philip well knew, the circus had a dark side, a side that people feared and distrusted, and he had to do his best to ensure that this should not work against him.

One of his more successful ventures was a 'bathing machine' that he installed in the River Thames at Vauxhall. He advertised it by swimming from Westminster Bridge to Blackfriars holding a flag erect in each hand. His footmen walked solemnly along the banks beside him, carrying towels monogrammed with the Astley arms. They were followed by Edward, proudly leading Gibraltar and Little Billy, and a full scale pipe band with riders on camels.

Charles and Veronica Hughes stood on Westminster Bridge watching this extraordinary sight. They had been drinking until seven o'clock in the morning the previous night and were suffering from terrible hangovers. Veronica's white teeth were yellowing, and Charles no longer bothered to shave. They were beaten and they knew it. Philip, through his incredible drive and inexhaustible energy, had won the battle for circus supremacy.

The 1780s were something of a honeymoon period for the Astleys. But in 1789 all this changed with the turmoil of the French Revolution. After years of unimaginable oppression, the starving peasants rose against the ruling classes and stormed the Bastille prison. Many members of the nobility had their heads cut off – and eventually King Louis XVI and Marie Antoinette were dragged to the guillotine too. Chaos reigned, nobody felt safe, and when the revolutionary mob even turned on its own leaders, all of France was plunged into a state of total terror.

When the Astley Amphitheatre was taken over as a

military barracks, John scuttled back to London. The good times were over, and the terrible scenes in Paris frightened him. Philip, however, was less timid, and did not miss an opportunity for a new production. Having grilled the rather pale-looking John for every gory detail, he staged full scale re-enactments of the revolution. He called his show *Paris in Uproar*. In an age before television or photography this was like watching the ten o'clock news. People had heard rumours of what was happening in Paris, but now, at Astley's Amphitheatre, they could watch it for themselves.

***

In 1793, when Britain went to war against France, Philip found himself deeply excited by the momentousness of world events – they rekindled memories of his days as a soldier. One day, without any warning, he suddenly declared to his family that he was going to rejoin his old regiment, the 15th Light Dragoons.

Sugar watched from her bedroom window at Hercules Hall as the love of her life rode off to war. Tears gushed down her cheeks; she felt that she had lost her darling husband forever. She loved him so much, and yet he barely spoke to her – he was always so busy. She felt old, worn-out, and lonely.

She also began to feel a little afraid; she knew that their amphitheatre had made many people very envious. No amount of success would get rid of their enemies; on the contrary, the more successful they were, the more certain people seemed to hate them. They were guarded by footmen, behind high gates, but as time went by Sugar felt more and more anxious about her and her son's safety.

Philip was sharp and knew how to protect his family and his amphitheatre, and by his publicity stunts and clever politics, he warded off the evil that lurked in the shadows. But John! Sugar shuddered. John – dear John. She loved her son but had no faith in him. He lacked authority. He lacked guile. He could be dangerously indiscreet. Even the artists didn't fully respect him. He pasted carefully worded notices backstage warning against such things as 'bad language, fighting, gentlemen in liquor and unbecoming behaviour – sky larking – which only tends to promote discord'. But without his father's iron rule, people laughed behind John's back.

What would become of them without Philip?

CHAPTER TWELVE

One morning, when he had been away with the army for about a year, Philip received a letter at his barracks in France. As soon as he saw the envelope, the address written in his son's familiar curly handwriting, he was worried; a letter from London was unlikely to be bringing good news.

'Dear father,' the letter began, 'I am deeply sorry to have to write with bad news. I wish I had good news. But I don't. It's very bad news in fact.' Philip read on with a sinking heart. His beloved Royal Grove amphitheatre, his beloved hall beside Westminster Bridge, his pride and joy, the most beautiful building in London, had burnt to the ground. John didn't say how the fire had started, but Philip could imagine it easily. A tinder-dry building, made from tarred ships masts, lit by candles and jets of gas, packed full of people every night. One spark, one cigarette... Philip's eyes filled with tears as he read that the building had burned for a whole day. Some of the horses had been killed in the flames.

From the date on the letter, which had taken a few days to reach him, Philip realised that the fire had happened a whole week before. He immediately made preparations to return to London. That night, as his coach rumbled and bounced along the potholed roads of northern France, he thought of his beautiful amphitheatre blazing against a night sky. The delight-ful sparkling lights, the fine velvet seats – all gone! The gorgeous stables, the carefully constructed warm-up area – all burnt to the ground! Once more he found himself crying. What made his pain worse was that it was his own son who had let the fire happen. 'John, John, the English Rose – an incapable fool!' Philip muttered to himself. He knew his son was a careless manager – he let workers smoke near the hay barns, and all too often candles were only half extinguished.

And then a terrible thought occurred to him, a thought that coursed down his spine and deep into the very pit of his stomach. Perhaps it wasn't John who was to blame... perhaps it was an arson attack! And Philip, in the dark of the jolting carriage, felt filled with rage as he pictured the thin, sinister face of Charles Hughes.

But when he returned to London, he was so overjoyed that Edward had saved his precious horses, Gibraltar and Little Billy, that he forgot all about his suspicions; and, instead of looking for someone to blame, he immediately set about rebuilding his amphitheatre.

'Now, ladies and gentlemen,' he told his performers, 'We must begin again. No deserters among you, I hope. You must stick by me, and I'll give you half-pay until we can begin performing once more.'

With his unique determination and energy, Philip not only managed to convert the old Lyceum Theatre on the Strand into a venue for his equestrian shows, he also began work on designing a new amphitheatre, built from a shipwreck he had found in a naval boat-yard.

Philip's performers and workers rallied round to help him in every way they could. His confident words, his energy and the complete faith he had in his work filled them with inspiration.

Secretly, Philip had no idea if he could make it happen again, and he often had nightmares in which evil people torched his buildings. But by day he communicated to his workers a wild faith that life would turn out all right if they all worked hard enough. And, more or less, he was right. The new building, which he grandly named the 'Amphitheatre of the Arts', was a huge success.

In art, as in life, war and horses were the themes which caught Philip's imagination. He staged some epic productions, including *Barn Munchhausen* and *The Siege of Troy*. 'Astley Productions', with their hugely expensive sets and huge casts, were like a sort of 18th-century Hollywood. John was put in charge of the front of the house, and he did this well. When shown to their seats, visitors to the new amphitheatre were treated to the most courteous attentions, and if they were lucky, a morsel of choice gossip as well. John even obliged his parents and got married. His wife was called Hannah.

***

During this time, an old friend, the owner of a small touring show, approached Philip and asked him if he could borrow Little Billy. In a moment of generosity, Philip had agreed. However, not long afterwards the friend went bankrupt, and all his possessions were sold off, including Little Billy. Philip was distraught. He spent weeks pacing the streets, looking everywhere for him. But Little Billy was nowhere to be found.

One day Edward and a group of workers were having a drink in a tavern in Piccadilly. It was a hot evening so they were sitting outside. Edward was watching the passers-by, as he always did, when, suddenly, across the dusty road, through horses' legs and turning carriage wheels, he spotted a familiar brown pony.

'Hey look, it's Little Billy I swear it!' he shouted as he jumped up, knocking over his glass. He ran across the road. He was so excited he was nearly knocked down by a cab, but he didn't care. He just wanted to see his old friend again.

'Come on Billy, shake my hand.' The pony lifted a hoof to Edward.

'It is him! Quick, John's in the theatre round the corner – he will know where Mr Astley is. Tell him to find his dad, quick!' he shouted to the others.

Edward waited with the pony while his friends ran off to find Philip. Meanwhile, Billy's new owner stumbled out of the tavern. Edward promised that Philip Astley himself would be there soon to pay in full for the pony, if only he would release him. The man willingly obliged, apparently pleased to share some of the celebrity of the famously gifted pony and his illustrious owner. The reunion of the two old artists was a very happy sight. Billy reared up and placed his two front legs on Philip's broad shoulders, and Philip, tears of joy streaming down his face, declared Billy the finest pony that had ever lived. Some people said that it was the last time they could remember Philip laughing so joyfully...

***

No matter how much success Philip enjoyed, he always wanted more. As soon as the Peace of Amiens was declared between France and Britain in 1802, he decided once again to set out for France, determined to reclaim his glorious amphitheatre in Paris.

But the war between Britain and France that followed the French Revolution was still not quite over. In May 1803 Napoleon Bonaparte, First Consul of the newly established 'French Republic', took control of all the French ports and declared every Englishman in France a prisoner of war.

Philip found himself captive in France.

Undaunted, he set about plotting his escape. One day, feigning illness, he persuaded his captors to allow him to take a ride in a carriage so that he could get some air. When they were on the road, Philip drew a pistol and held it to the driver's head, commanding that he be driven to the French border. The driver was so intimidated by this ferocious Englishman with his loud voice and bear-like stature, that he did as he was told. Philip reached the frontier and managed to escape through Holland.

But he came home to terrible news: not only had his amphitheatre once again burned to the ground; the fire had killed his mother-in-law and more than fifty of his best horses. Far worse than anything, though, was the news that Sugar, too, had died the week before.

Philip was full of anguish. His beloved Sugar gone, his business wrecked. He was wracked with guilt that he had failed to be a loving husband. He was now alone in the world, and he became convinced that his enemies, the shadowy figures that haunted his dreams, were catching up with him. This terrible paranoia burnt away at his soul, and fuelled the ambition that would not let him rest; he began at once to build his third amphitheatre.

Designed by the fashionable scene painter John Henderson Grieve, who had also worked on Covent Garden, the new amphitheatre was painted green and crimson. Fluted pillars, inlaid with mirrors and decorated with gold, supported the colossal roof, and ten gleaming chandeliers illuminated the vast internal 'arena'. Its beauty took even Philip's breath away.

Philip was still the little boy sitting in his father's workshop, vowing that he would one day achieve greatness, still the runaway, still the soldier throwing himself into the water to save the drowning horse. He was still the star of the Three Hats Inn all those years ago. He was still Sergeant-Major Philip Astley, throwing his heart at the world and proving at every turn that he was the best.

The life of a showman is a hard one, because a

showman is never happy until he is the best, and once he is the best – then there will always be someone out there wishing him bad luck with all their might. Philip's struggle to prove himself never ended.

Even after that third rebuilding of the amphitheatre he didn't stop. He bought another theatre on Newcastle Street, off the Strand, and in 1807 opened it as the Olympic Pavilion. And over the next few years, he went on to build nineteen more amphitheatres across Britain, Ireland and Europe. As he grew older he only pushed himself harder. 'I am no man of straw!' he used to say of himself, and no one could argue with that.

He died in Paris, at the age of seventy-two, of a painful affliction known as gout; and was buried in the cemetery of Père Lachaise. John died, childless, a year later and was buried next to his father. Hannah had his headstone engraved with the words 'The Once Rose of Paris'.

This is the end of the life of Sergeant-Major Philip Astley. We can only wonder at his phenomenal ability to make his dreams come true. Perhaps his relentless ambition obscured the simple desire to be happy. But at least Philip could take pride in having fulfilled his vision. By the time he died, Astley's Amphitheatre had become a household name. Circuses like Astley's were built in hundreds of towns and cities, and before long there were circus shows in every country in the world.

Two of the original posters used to advertise Astley's circus in the early 19th century

NOVEL FEATURE AT
ASTLEYS ROYAL AMPHITHEATRE
THE RING & STAGE COMBINED

TO FORM ONE VAST ARENA
IN WHICH THE
BATTLE OF THE ALMA
IS PERFORMED
EVERY EVENING
LESSEE AND MANAGER, MR Wm COOKE.

J. GIBBS & CO LITH 3 SNOW HILL LONDON

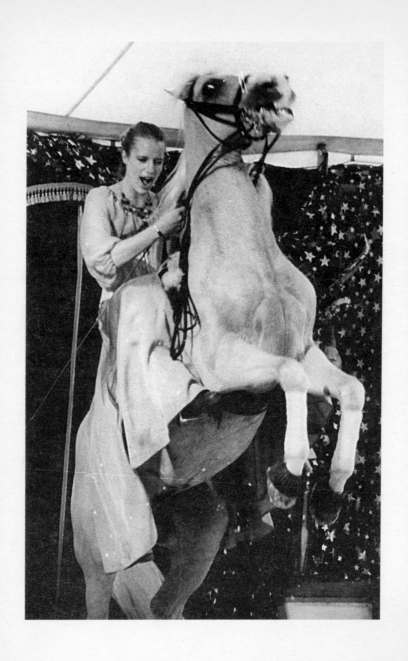

✳About the author✳

Nell Stroud was born in 1973. Her first book, *Josser*,
was published in 1999. She is the co-founder of
Giffords Circus, based in the Cotswolds.

GIFFORDS CIRCUS

WINNER OF THE PRESTIGIOUS
JERWOOD CIRCUS AWARD IN 2002

'Giffords Circus fulfils every childhood fantasy
of what a travelling circus should be'
Telegraph Magazine

'Nell Gifford...stands out as an exotic creature
in a world of exotic creatures'
The Times

**Giffords circus tours the Cotswolds
every summer from May to September.
For information call
Giffords on 07818 058 384
For bookings call the
Everyman Theatre on 01242 572573**

www.giffordscircus.com

OTHER TITLES IN THE **WHO WAS?** SERIES:

DAVID LIVINGSTONE
The Legendary Explorer
Amanda Mitchison

No one could have imagined that David, a poor Glasgow cotton-mill worker, would grow up to become a hero of his time — the great explorer of an unknown world.

   This is the incredible story of David Livingstone – the tough man of Victorian Britain who would stop at nothing in his determination to explore Africa, even if it meant dragging his wife and children along with him. He trekked hundreds of miles through dangerous territory, encountering killer-ants, lions and cannibals – sometimes with terrible consequences...

ISBN: 1-904095-30-5

MADAME TUSSAUD

Waxwork Queen of the French Revolution

Tony Thorne

Young Marie first showed a talent for life-modelling as a teenager in Paris. Sent to live in the royal household, she started sculpting famous figures, including King Louis XVI himself.

When the Revolution struck, Marie was torn. She understood why the poor had risen up in protest, but she couldn't forget the kindnesses of the King. Should she stick with the royalists, or go over to the rebels' side?

The French Revolution, as it turned out, was only the start of Marie's adventures. This is the amazing story of the woman who founded London's celebrated waxwork museum, Madame Tussaud's.

ISBN: 1-904095-29-1

QUEEN VICTORIA
The Woman who Ruled the World
Kate Hubbard

Victoria was just 18 when she was crowned Queen in 1837 – a tiny figure with a will of iron. Never was there so queenly a queen. She made Britain great, and the people loved her for it.

In 1861 tragedy struck, when her husband Albert died. The little Queen loved dogs and cream cakes and the troops who fought her wars, but most of all she loved Albert. Dumb with grief, she hid herself away. Suddenly it seemed the woman who had made the monarchy so strong would destroy it. Could anyone persuade Victoria to be Queen again?

ISBN: 1-904095-32-1

WILLIAM SHAKESPEARE

The Mystery of the World's Greatest Playwright

Rupert Christiansen

Everyone has heard of plays like Macbeth and A Midsummer Night's Dream. But why do we know so little about the man who wrote them? Who exactly was William Shakespeare from Stratford-upon-Avon, and why do so many people believe that he was not the person he seemed to be?

This book is an exciting detective story, which goes back over four hundred years to the dramatic events of the reign of Queen Elizabeth I and explores the way that a brilliant and ambitious young man was caught up in a violent world of murder, revenge and treason.

ISBN: 1-904095-34-8

FLORENCE NIGHTINGALE
The Lady and the Lamp
Charlotte Moore

Even as a little girl, Florence Nightingale knew she was different. Unlike the rest of her family, she wasn't interested in fancy clothes or grand parties. She knew God wanted her to do something different, something important... but what?

In 1854, shocking everyone, she set off to help save the thousands of British soldiers injured in the disastrous Crimean war. Nothing could have prepared her for the horror of the army hospital, where soldiers writhed in agony as rats scuttled around them on the blood-stained floor.

But Florence set to work, and became the greatest nurse the world had ever seen...

ISBN: 1-904095-33-X

ADA LOVELACE

The Computer Wizard of Victorian England

Lucy Lethbridge

Daughter of the famous romantic poet Lord Byron, Ada Lovelace was a child prodigy. Brilliant at maths, she read numbers like most people read words.

In 1834 she came to the attention of Charles Babbage, a scientist and techno-whizz who had just built an amazing new 'THINKING MACHINE'. Ada and Mr Babbage started working together – a perfect partnership which bore fruit in the most important invention of the modern world, THE COMPUTER!

ISBN: 1-904095-52-6

In case of difficulty in purchasing any Short Books
title through normal channels, please contact
BOOKPOST Tel: 01624 836000
Fax: 01624 837033
email: bookshop@enterprise.net
www.bookpost.co.uk
Please quote ref. 'Short Books'